The Official
SUNDERLAND
Association Football Club Annual 2008

Written by Rob Mason, SAFC Publications Officer.
Pages 20 & 21 by Barbara Mason.

A Grange Publication

© 2007. Published by Grange Communications Ltd., Edinburgh, under licence from Sunderland Football Club. Printed in the EU.

ISBN 978-1-905426-93-5

£6.99

Coca-Cola
CHAMPIONSHIP
CHAMPIONS 2007 SUNDE

CONTENTS

Roy joins in training.

ROY KEANE

Sunderland's manager is Roy Keane. He was one of the most famous players of his generation and became a manager for the first time when he took over at Sunderland in August 2006. At the time Sunderland had just been relegated from the Premier League and had begun the season badly.

Keane completely changed things at Sunderland. He brought a lot of new faces in, got the best out of the existing players he kept; in some cases by changing their position such as with Nyron Nosworthy. By the end of the season he saw his team do what he had done so often throughout his own playing days – win a trophy!

Sunderland won the Championship in 2007, finishing top of the table after a brilliant final day 5-0 away win after losing only once in the league between New Year's Day and the end of the season.

Named manager of the month in February and March, Roy then won the Championship manager of the season award and while he is always ready to give the credit for any success to his players there is no doubt that he fully deserved the manager of the year award as a reward.

Roy Keane with Sunderland player of the century Charlie Hurley.

KAV ON TARGET

New boy Graham Kavanagh gets his first goal for Sunderland in a 3-0 win over Leeds at Elland Road.

CHAMPIONS OF THE CHAMPIONSHIP

Coventry (A) lost 2-1

Birmingham City (h) lost 1-0

Plymouth Argyle (h) lost 3-2

Southend Utd (a) lost 3-1

Bury (Carling Cup) (a) lost 2-0

WBA (h) won 2-0

POSITION AT END OF THE MONTH **23rd**

Sunderland began the season disastrously! The first four league games were lost despite the Lads taking the lead in two of them. The fourth of those fixtures at Southend saw Jon Stead score so late in injury time it was barely a consolation as the newly promoted Shrimpers beat sorry Sunderland 3-1. The one bright spark was the debut of the Spaniard Arnau who came on as a substitute. Three days later Arnau was given his first start... and was sent off after just three minutes as Sunderland lost to Bury who were bottom of League Two. Following on from the previous season's relegation with the lowest number of points in Premier League history it was a terrible start but from that moment on the only way was up!

Niall Quinn was trying to manage the team as well as being Chairman and after the Bury game he had everybody guessing when he announced that a world class figure was about to take over as manager. Come the next match and live on TV Sunderland played their best football in ages to defeat unbeaten West Brom while up in the stands sat the world class figure set to be appointed manager the following morning...Roy Keane.

WATCHING BRIEF

Would-be manager Roy Keane watches Sunderland beat West Brom at home before his official appointment at the Stadium of Light.

SEPTEMBER

Derby Co. (a) won 2-1	
Leeds Utd (a) won 3-0	
Leicester City (h) drew 1-1	
Ipswich Town (a) lost 3-1	
Sheffield Wed (h) won 1-0	

POSITION AT END OF THE MONTH — 14th

Huge numbers of supporters followed Sunderland to Derby as the 'Roy-volution' got under way. The new manager had signed six players already and when one of them, Ross Wallace, scored Sunderland's second goal in two minutes as Sunderland turned around a half time deficit the 'Magic Carpet' ride Niall Quinn had spoken about was cleared for take off.

THE BOSS
Keane takes charge of his first game against Derby at Pride Park.

Next stop was Leeds where Sunderland played like the champions they were destined to be. Quick, accurate passing, players running off the ball and spectacular goals were something Sunderland supporters had mainly only seen other teams do for the previous year and they lapped up the chance to see the Black Cats purr.

Toby Hysen got a great goal against Leicester in Roy Keane's first home game and although there was a defeat at Ipswich the month ended with a win over Sheffield Wednesday thanks to Grant Leadbitter's first goal for his home town team.

OCTOBER

Preston NE (a) lost 4-1	
Stoke City (a) lost 2-1	
Barnsley (h) won 2-0	
Hull City (a) won 1-0	
Cardiff City (h) lost 2-1	

POSITION AT END OF THE MONTH — 15th

An international break meant a fortnight's gap to the next match but when it came around Sunderland were hammered by Preston and then slipped up again at Stoke where they lost after scoring first – something that wouldn't happen again all season.

Up to this stage the only late goal Sunderland had scored was that almost worthless effort at Southend but the new Sunderland started scoring late goals almost as a matter of routine with the wins over Barnsley and Hull coming from goals in the final few minutes.

Cardiff were top of the table when they came to the Stadium of Light at Halloween but there were no treats for the home fans as two goals from former Newcastle player Michael Chopra did the trick. Sunderland would have the last laugh though.

DEBUT DELIGHT
New signing Ross Wallace scores the winning goal over the Rams in a 2-1 win at Pride Park.

NOVEMBER

- Norwich City (a) lost 1-0
- Southampton (h) drew 1-1
- Colchester Utd (h) won 3-1
- Wolves (a) drew 1-1
- QPR (a) won 2-1

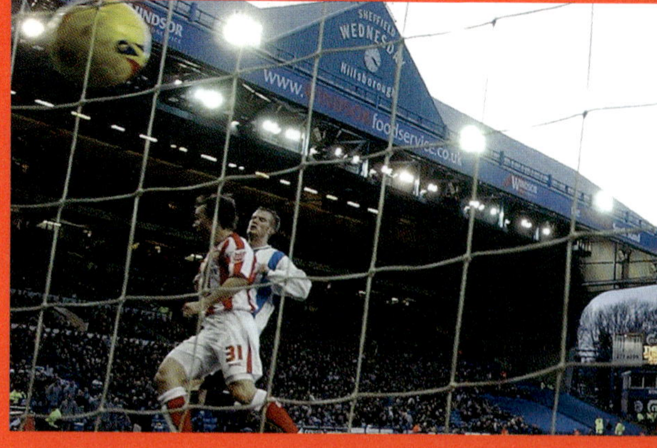

HILLSBOROUGH HIGH
Connolly is on target again, this time the third goal in a 4-2 win over Sheffield Wednesday.

14th

November started and ended away from home. Somehow Sunderland lost a game they dominated at Norwich but by the time they won much more handsomely than the 2-1 scoreline suggests at QPR they had comfortably beaten Colchester and taken draws from the two teams destined to lose out in the play off semi finals.

DECEMBER

- Norwich City (h) won 1-0
- Luton Town (h) won 2-1
- Burnley (a) drew 2-2
- Crystal Palace (a) lost 1-0
- Leeds Utd (h) won 2-0
- Preston NE (h) lost 1-0

LATE RELIEF
Striker David Connolly nets an injury-time equaliser against Burnley at Turf Moor.

12th

Solid home wins over Norwich and Luton were followed by a fighting draw at Burnley where spectacular late shots from David Connolly and Grant Leadbitter extended an unbeaten run to seven games but that came to an end on a foggy London night at Crystal Palace just before Christmas.

It was better on Boxing Day when Leeds became the first of eight teams Sunderland did the 'double' over. Only Preston did the 'double' over Sunderland and in fact they made it a treble by knocking Sunderland out of the FA Cup a week later.

- Leicester City (a) won 2-0
- Preston NE (FA Cup) (a) lost 1-0
- Ipswich Town (h) won 1-0
- Sheffield Wed (a) won 4-2
- Crystal Palace (h) drew 0-0

POSITION AT END OF THE MONTH

9th

New Year's Day saw the start of an unbeaten league run that would stretch to April 21st. Still in the bottom half of the table when 2007 kicked off Sunderland would be top of the league by the time the run came to an end. Sunderland had never gone so far into a calendar year without a league defeat.

In fact Preston completed that 'treble' with an FA Cup win but Sunderland played over half the match with ten men and were looking much better than the previous tip to Preston, not least as new signings Jonny Evans and Carlos Edwards made their debuts. Edwards would be consistently excellent on the wing and score some great great goals while Evans, on loan from Manchester United would become Young Player of the Year.

The Player of the Year would be Nyron Nosworthy and in the next game – against Ipswich – he would be transformed from full back to centre back. Despite winning 4-2 at Sheffield Wednesday the manager was unhappy with late goals being given away. The players got the message... they didn't concede another one for 450 minutes.

PRICELESS

Liam Miller heads an injury-time winner over Derby at the Stadium of Light, a victory which manager Roy Keane later described as the defining moment in the season.

- Coventry City (h) won 2-0
- Plymouth Argyle (a) won 2-0
- Southend Utd (h) won 4-0
- Birmingham City (a) drew 1-1
- Derby Co (h) won 2-1

POSITION AT END OF THE MONTH

4th

Three solid wins that added to the goalless draw with Palace at the end of January meant four clean sheets in a row and by the time Southend had been despatched with the help of Stern John's first two goals for the club, Sunderland had climbed into the Play Off places for the first time. The next three fixtures were against the three teams then in the top three places so Sunderland knew they were in for a challenge... but it was one they went into full of confidence.

First up was Birmingham away. Birmingham eventually finished runners up to Sunderland and although this game was drawn City had to be thankful for a last minute equaliser after a scintillating Sunderland performance that featured something fans would get used to – a blistering goal from Carlos Edwards.

February ended with top of the table Derby at the Stadium of Light. The Rams had been the opposition in Roy Keane's first game as manager and this would also be a defining moment. To begin with supporters had to get over the shock of seeing Sunderland awarded their first penalty in 63 games stretching back almost a year and a half! Top scorer David Connolly tucked that away only for County to level with a classy goal from Giles Barnes. Having suffered a last minute goal at Birmingham though this time it was the Black Cats' turn to enjoy a goal in the dying seconds as midfielder Liam Miller glanced home a Grant Leadbitter cross to win a dramatic game.

CORNERSTONE Grant Leadbitter salutes the Sunderland faithful after grabbing an 87th-minute winner at Southampton.

MARCH

WBA (a) won 2-1

Barnsley (a) won 2-0

Stoke City (h) drew 2-2

Hull City (h) won 2-0

Cardiff City (a) won 1-0

Sunderland made it seven points out of nine against the top three with a 2-1 win at West Brom more comfortable than the scoreline suggests and then the fans took over at Barnsley where another three points saw Sunderland move up to third place.

It needed another last minute goal, this time by Daryl Murphy to force a draw with Stoke before a comfortable win over Hull lifted the lads into the automatic promotion places for the first time.

March ended at Cardiff. When the sides had met in the north east five months to the day earlier Cardiff had been top of the table and beat Sunderland 2-1 but on this occasion a Ross Wallace free kick won the points for the Wearsiders and just about ended the Welshmen's play off hopes. On the way home a plane load of Sunderland supporters were stranded at Bristol airport when a flight was cancelled. Niall Quinn was on the same flight and paid for taxis to get the stranded passengers home.

WINNER

The roll continues, this time with a win at rivals West Brom as Dwight Yorke congratulates fellow T&T man Stern John on netting Sunderland's second goal at the Hawthorns.

APRIL

2nd

Wolves (h) won 2-1

Southampton (a) won 2-1

QPR (h) won 2-1

Colchester Utd (a) lost 3-1

Burnley (h) won 3-2

POSITION AT END OF THE MONTH   **2nd**

Easter is traditionally a time when leagues are won and lost and Sunderland had a cracking Easter. Former manager Mick McCarthy's new side Wolves put up a good fight at Sunderland on Easter Saturday but were beaten 2-1 and when Sunderland were live on TV at Southampton come Easter Monday the lads had the chance of going to the top of the league. Trailing 1-0 with thirteen minutes left didn't stop them. Carlos Edwards hit one of his 'specials' and Grant Leadbitter made the Black Cats into top cats with another screamer. Having got the fans home in taxis in the last away game this time it was the team bus who picked up stranded fans to drive them home after dropping the players off at the airport!

Another late Leadbitter winner kept the points flowing against QPR but on April 21st something happened that no one had seen in 2007- Sunderland lost a league game. It was the furthest into a calendar year that Sunderland had ever gone without league defeat and it came in a 3-1 reverse at Colchester but the lads knew that with two more games to go their destiny was still in their own hands.

The Championship's biggest crowd of the season, 44,448 attended for a Friday night game live on TV to see the crunch game with Burnley. The visitors had a host of ex SAFC personnel and inevitably it was one of them – Andy Gray – who scored with a penalty. That helped Burnley to go from 1-0 down to 2-1 up later in the game but David Connolly showed his character to net from a penalty after having an earlier spot kick saved but the best was still to come.

Danny Collins had been a defensive rock all season and when he won the ball on his own goal line he started a move that led to one of the best goals Sunderland have ever scored, slick passing from one end of the pitch to the other teeing up Edwards who struck a shot from 30 yards that flew into the top corner for a goal fit to win any game and Sunderland's promotion was made certain when Derby lost at Crystal Palace the following Sunday.

THANK YOU

Boss Keane applauds the Sunderland supporters after the club's last home game of the campaign, a thrilling 3-2 win over Burnley which edged the club nearer promotion.

CHAMPIONS

Sunderland clinch the Championship trophy with a 5-0 win at Luton, after Birmingham lose 1-0 at Preston.

PARTY TIME

The Champagne corks are popping in the Sunderland dressing room at Kenilworth Road as the players celebrate their title.

MAY

Luton (a) won 5-0

1st

POSITION AT END OF THE MONTH

Wrapping up a Championship with a 5-0 away win is the mark of true champions. Sunderland were 2-0 up within six minutes at Luton and the goals just kept coming but it was a goal at Preston where North End beat Birmingham City that combined to ensure Sunderland finished the season where they deserved to be... at the top.

Thousands of Sunderland fans had taken over Luton's Kenilworth Road and although the players had to wait until the following day to get their hands on the trophy the emotional scenes at the end of the match showed exactly what it means for a Sunderland supporter to be top of the league!

WE DID IT

Sunderland clinch promotion to the Premiership without kicking a ball! Derby's 2-0 defeat at Crystal Palace on Sunday April 29 confirms the Black Cats' return to the top flight.

TROPHY

Skipper Dean Whitehead finally gets his hands on the Championship trophy in a formal presentation to the players at Seaham Hall.

TEN THINGS
TO KNOW ABOUT SUNDERLAND'S
PLAYER OF THE YEAR

1. HIS NICKNAME IS 'NUGSY' "BECAUSE MY DAD ALWAYS SAYS MY HEAD LOOKS LIKE A NUGGET" ACCORDING TO NYRON HIMSELF.

2. HE STARTED HIS CAREER AT GILLINGHAM.

3. HE JOINED SUNDERLAND ON A FREE TRANSFER IN THE SUMMER OF 2005.

4. WHEN HE SIGNED GILLINGHAM HAD JUST BEEN RELEGATED AND SUNDERLAND HAD JUST BEEN PROMOTED.

5. HE WAS A RIGHT BACK UNTIL ROY KEANE CONVERTED HIM TO CENTRE BACK.

6. AT GILLINGHAM HE OCCASIONALLY PLAYED AS A STRIKER.

7. HE ONCE SCORED TWICE AGAINST CRYSTAL PALACE WHEN PLAYING FOR GILLINGHAM.

8. HIS BROTHER DWAYNE HAS PRESENTED TV PROGRAMMES ON SKY.

9. HE IS A LONDONER.

10. SUNDERLAND SUPPORTERS SIMPLY LOVE NYRON NOSWORTHY.

NYRON NOSWORTHY

THE MIGHTY QUINN

Sunderland's chairman is Niall Quinn. What a chairman to have. Niall is a mega hero to Sunderland fans. He has played for the club, been manager and is now chairman. How amazing is that?

Back in 1996 Niall became Sunderland's record signing when he signed from Manchester City just as Sunderland were about to play their first ever match in the Premiership. He scored twice in a 4-1 away win in his first full game but unfortunately was soon injured and missed most of the season. Determined to do his best for Sunderland Quinn came back before he was fully fit at the end of the season but couldn't stop the team being relegated.

Sunderland kicked off the following season at their fantastic new ground, the Stadium of Light. Niall netted the first ever goal there and would later score the first hat trick at the ground. At the end of the season he became the first Sunderland player to score twice at Wembley. That was in the 1998 Play Off final which has been voted Wembley's greatest ever game. It ended 4-4 after extra time only for Sunderland to lose on penalties although Niall scored from his spot kick. Always an inspirational person, Niall played a big part in helping everyone get over the disappointment and the next three seasons were fantastic.

A record 105 points were won as Sunderland won promotion and for the next two years Sunderland finished 7th in the Premier League with Niall and his fellow striker Kevin Phillips the best strike partnership in the land. Not only that but in both of those seasons Sunderland won away to local rivals Newcastle and the only man to score in both of those victories was of course...Niall Quinn!

Injury forced Niall to retire in 2002 but not before he organised a benefit match at the Stadium of Light between Sunderland and his international side The Republic of Ireland. At the time he was his country's all time record goal scorer and he played part of that game for both sides on what was a wonderful night of carnival football shared by the supporters of Sunderland and Ireland who mixed together to celebrate a joint hero who then gave all the money raised from the match to charities with hospitals in Sunderland and the Republic of Ireland's capital Dublin benefiting.

All of this made 'The Mighty Quinn' a massive hero in Sunderland but then with Sunderland struggling badly in 2006 Niall got together a group of people, mainly from Ireland, to take over the club. Calling themselves Drumaville, the group gave Sunderland a new start. Niall took over as manager himself for a while until he could attract a world class manager. Sunderland lost the first five games of the season but dramatically beat West Brom live on TV in Niall's last match as manager before Roy Keane took over leaving Quinn to concentrate on being the sort of chairman that every set of supporters wish their club could have.

WHITE WATER RAFTING

Sunderland's squad sometimes have unusual training sessions and we'll show you a few more of them later in your annual. One of the stranger things Sunderland's players have got up to is to go white water rafting. Sometimes you hear of footballers who have to 'keep their heads above water' or are experiencing a 'sinking feeling' but the squad who went on this expedition were undoubtedly 'on the crest of a wave!'

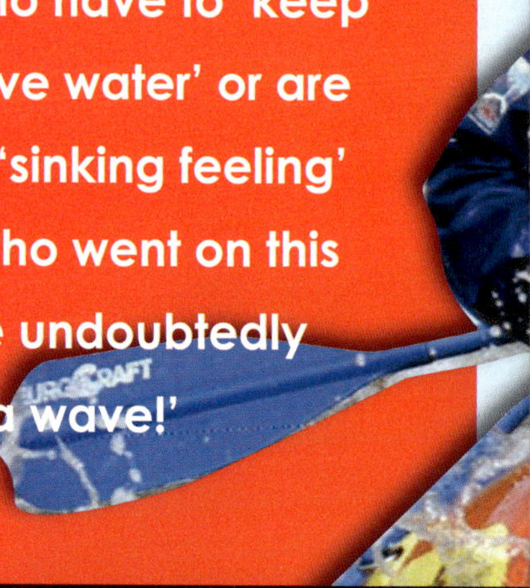

SAMSON SHOWS YOU HOW TO MAKE THE PURR-FECT BIRTHDAY CARD

It's always extra special if you take the trouble to make someone a birthday card. Samson shows you how easy it is.

You will need:

1 sheet of white card
2 sheets of white paper
coloured pencils or felt tips
a glue-stick
scissors (be careful)
sellotape.

Step 2

Draw a picture of Samson to go on the front of the card. This will need to be about ¾ of the height of your card. You can use the template shown or draw your own.

Step 4

Stick your picture of Samson onto the front of the card leaving a gap at the top of the card where you can write Samson says ... in large letters.

Step 1

Start by neatly folding your sheet of white card in half.

Step 3

Colour your picture of Samson in with your pencils or felt tips and cut him out as carefully as you can.

Step 5

Inside the card is a surprise... a pop-up black cat!
Draw his shape on a piece of paper, or use the template.
Colour him in and cut him out.

Template 1

Template 2

Step 6

Cut a narrow strip of paper about 2.5 cm wide and 20cm long. Make it into a ring and sellotape it together.

Step 7

Glue or sellotape the paper ring to the back of your picture of the cat.

Step 8

Stick a piece of sellotape through the ring you have made and then stick the ring to the centre of the inside of your card. This is so that the pop-up cat stands out from the card.

Write Happy Birthday along the top and when you open the card you should see the black cat leap out!

SUNDERLAND LEGENDS

MONTY

Jimmy Montgomery hasn't just played more games for Sunderland than anyone else in the club's history – he has played over 150 times more than anyone else. A brilliant goalkeeper, 'Monty' earned world wide fame for making the greatest save ever made at Wembley stadium. His fantastic reflex double save came in the 1973 FA Cup final when Sunderland beat Leeds 1-0 in one of the most famous cup finals of all time. However anyone who watched Monty week in week out knew that Monty made miraculous saves all the time and as the song went 'Come on without, Come on within, You'll not see nothing like the Mighty Jim!"

THE KING

Charlie Hurley was voted Sunderland's 'Player of the Century' when the club celebrated 100 years in 1979. The captain of Sunderland's first ever promotion team in 1964 – when Charlie was runner up as Footballer of the Year to Bobby Moore – Hurley was known then as he is now, simply as 'The King.'

A centre half who won everything in the air and was superb with the ball at his feet, Charlie did something no other centre half had ever done before. He started going forward for corners. Nowadays every centre back in the world does that routinely but when 'The King' strode forward against Sheffield United in 1962 no one had ever seen anything like it. Crowds didn't chant much as they do now – they just cheered and roared mainly – but from then on every time Sunderland won a corner the whole ground would chant 'Charlie, Charlie.'

HIGHEST EVER SCORER

Bobby Gurney scored 228 goals for Sunderland. 31 of these came in 1935-36 when the Lads became champions of England for the sixth time. A year later Gurney headed Sunderland's first ever goal at Wembley. That came in the 1937 FA Cup final as Sunderland won the cup for the first time beating Preston North End 3-1.

Gurney was famous for chasing lost causes. He would never give anything up and a lot of his goals were considered 'impossible' goals that no one else would have scored. Often he would score from ridiculously narrow angles or late in the game because if any player ever 'played for the shirt' it was Bobby Gurney, a true Sunderland hero.

HIGHEST EVER LEAGUE SCORER

Charlie Buchan scored 222 goals for Sunderland. Although this was six fewer than Gurney later managed, Buchan's 209 in the league made him the club's highest all time league scorer. Buchan played for Sunderland between 1911 and 1925 winning the title in 1912-13 and playing in Sunderland's first FA Cup final that year. Wembley wasn't built until a decade later but once it was open Charlie was England's centre forward in the first ever international there.

PLAYER PROFILES

TREVOR CARSON

Position	Goalkeeper
Birthdate	5.3.88
Birthplace	Downpatrick, Northern Ireland

Other clubs None. Signed from Killyleagh Boys
International honours: Northern Ireland U21
Did you know? Trevor sometimes played as a striker at U18 level.

Position	Central defender or left back
Birthdate	6.8.80
Birthplace	Chester

Other clubs Chester, Buckley Town, Vauxhall Motors (Loan)
International honours: Wales
Did you know? Danny has played for Wales at cricket as well as football and has also played semi professional football for England.

DANNY COLLINS

DAVID CONNOLLY

Position	Striker
Birthdate	6.6.77
Birthplace	Willesden

Other clubs Watford, Feyenoord, Wolves (loan), Excelsior (loan), Wimbledon, West Ham, Leicester City, Wigan Athletic.
International honours Republic of Ireland
Did you know? David used to play alongside Kevin Phillips at Watford.

Position	Right wing
Birthdate	24.10.78
Birthplace	Port of Spain, Trinidad

Other clubs Patna Utd, Queens Park (Trinidad not Scotland), Defence Force, Wrexham, Luton Town
International honours Trinidad and Tobago
Did you know? Carlos played in the 2006 World Cup finals.

CARLOS EDWARDS

Position   Right back
Birthdate   12.9.89
Birthplace   Shotley Bridge, Co. Durham
Other clubs   None
International honours: England U17
Did you know? Michael's first outing was for the first team at Darlington in July 2007.

MICHAEL KAY

MARTON FULOP

Position   Goalkeeper
Birthdate   3.5.83
Birthplace   Budapest
Other clubs MTK Hungaria, BKV Elore (loan), Bodajk, Tottenham Hotspur, Chesterfield (loan), Coventry City (loan)
International honours Hungary
Did you know? Marton was the first player ever to be transferred from Spurs to Sunderland.

Position   Defender
Birthdate   3.3.89
Birthplace   Dublin
Other clubs None
International honours Republic of Ireland U17
Did you know? After an injury hit 2006-07 Gavin was given an extra six months at the club to earn a professional contract.

GAVIN DONOGHUE

STERN JOHN

Position   Striker
Birthdate   30.10.76
Birthplace   Tunapuna, Trinidad.
Other clubs Malta Carib Alcans, Carolina Dynamo, New Orleans Riverboat Gamblers, Columbus Crew, Nottingham Forest, Birmingham City, Coventry City, Derby County (loan).
International honours Trinidad and Tobago
Did you know? Stern has played over 100 times for Trinidad and Tobago.

Position   Midfield
Birthdate   3.12.73
Birthplace   Dublin
Other clubs Home Farm, Middlesbrough, Stoke City, Cardiff City, Wigan Athletic.
International honours Republic of Ireland
Did you know? Kav played in the 2006 League Cup final for Wigan.

GRAHAM KAVANAGH

Position   Midfield
Birthdate   7.1.86
Birthplace   Sunderland
Other clubs Rotherham United (loan)
International honours England U20
Did you know? Grant's schoolboy hero was Paul Scholes

GRANT LEADBITTER

LIAM MILLER

Position   Midfield
Birthdate   13.2.81
Birthplace   Cork
Other clubs Celtic, Aarhus (Denmark, loan) Manchester United, Leeds (loan
International honours Republic of Ireland
Did you know? Liam's best pal at Sunderland is Ross Wallace.

Position   Striker or left midfield
Birthdate   15.3.83
Birthplace   Waterford
Other clubs Luton Town, Waterford
International honours: Republic of Ireland
Did you know? Daryl made his international debut in New York Giants' American Football stadium.

DARYL MURPHY

Position   Central defender or right back
Birthdate   11.10.80
Birthplace   Brixton, London
Other clubs Gillingham
International honours None
Did you know? Nyron's brother Dwayne hopes to make it as a TV presenter.

NYRON NOSWORTHY

Position   Striker
Birthdate   25.7.88
Birthplace   Dublin
Other clubs Arsenal, Falkirk (loan)
International honours Republic of Ireland
Did you know? Anthony's only appearance for Arsenal was against Sunderland.

ANTHONY STOKES

STANISLAV VARGA

Position Central defender
Birthdate 8.10.72
Birthplace Bresov, Slovakia
Other clubs Tatran Presov, Slovan Bratislava, WBA (loan) Celtic
International honours Slovakia
Did you know? 'Stan' is in his second spell with Sunderland.

Position Left wing
Birthdate 23.5.85
Birthplace Dundee
Other clubs Celtic
International honours Scotland U21
Did you know? Roy Keane was Wallace's schoolboy hero

ROSS WALLACE

DARREN WARD

Position Goalkeeper
Birthdate 11.5.74
Birthplace Worksop
Other clubs Mansfield, Notts County, Nottingham Forest and Norwich City
International honours. Wales
Did you know? Darren has kept goal for the Magpies with Sam Allardyce as manager...at Notts County!

Position Midfield
Birthdate 12.1.82
Birthplace Abingdon, Oxford
Other clubs Oxford United
International honours None
Did you know? Dean has been in the PFA divisional select XI in three out of the last four seasons.

DEAN WHITEHEAD

DWIGHT YORKE

Position Midfield or striker
Birthdate 3.12.71
Birthplace Canaan, Tobago
Other clubs St. Clair's (Tobago), Aston Villa, Manchester United, Blackburn Rovers, Birmingham City, Sydney FC (Australia).
International honours Trinidad and Tobago
Did you know? Dwight is a massive cricket fan and a great friend of West Indies' superstar Brian Lara.

SUMMER SIGNINGS

Roy Keane spent the summer shopping for players to strengthen Sunderland ahead of stepping up to the Premier League. He went out to buy players who have ability, the right attitude and a hunger to do well in the game. Wherever possible the manager also looked for players in their early twenties, players with a bit of experience and not just potential but with their best years just ahead of them, years they will hope to spend doing well at Sunderland.

CRAIG GORDON

Position: Goalkeeper
Signed from: Hearts
Transfer fee: up to £9m
Birthdate: 31.12.82
Birthplace: Edinburgh
Other clubs: -
Did you know: Craig became Britain's most expensive goalkeeper and Sunderland's record signing when he joined in August?

KIERAN RICHARDSON

Position: Midfield or left back
Signed from: Manchester United
Transfer fee: Undisclosed
Birthdate: 21.10 84
Birthplace: Greenwich, London
Other clubs: West Ham and loan to West Brom.
International honours: England
Did you know: Kieran scored twice on his full England debut?

DICKSON ETUHU

Position: Centre midfield
Signed from: Norwich City
Transfer fee: £1.5m
Birthdate: 8.6.82
Birthplace: Kano, Nigeria
Other clubs: Manchester City and Preston North End.
Did you know: Dickson played in the same school team in London as Nyron Nosworthy?

GREG HALFORD

Position: Right back
Signed from: Reading
Transfer fee: £3m
Birthdate: 8.12.84
Birthplace: Chelmsford
Other clubs: Colchester United
International honours: England U20
Did you know: 6' 5" Greg is the tallest outfield player ever to play for Sunderland?

MICHAEL CHOPRA

Position: Striker
Signed from: Cardiff City
Transfer fee: Up to £5m
Birthdate: 23.12.83
Birthplace: Newcastle
Other clubs: Newcastle plus loans at Watford, Nottingham Forest and Barnsley.
International honours: England U20
Did you know: Michael once scored two goals for England U20s against Italy at the Stadium of Light?

RUSSELL ANDERSON

Position: Central defender
Signed from: Aberdeen
Transfer fee: £1m
Birthdate: 25.10.78
Birthplace: Aberdeen
Other clubs: None
International honours: Scotland
Did you know: When Russell signed for Sunderland he gave a fee he was due to Aberdeen to help with the youth programme he had benefited from?

PAUL MCSHANE

Position: Defender
Signed from: WBA
Transfer fee: Up to £2.5m
Birthdate: 6.1.86
Birthplace: Wicklow, Republic of Ireland
Other clubs: Manchester United plus loans with Walsall and Brighton
Did you know: Paul was a team mate of Kieran Richardson's when Man Utd won the FA Youth Cup in 2003?

RACE YOUR FRIENDS TO THE PREMIER LEAGUE TITLE.

To play this game you need:
A dice.
A counter for each player – preferably different colours to match the team you are, e.g. red for Sunderland, blue for Chelsea, white for Spurs.

Arsenal, Newcastle, Man Utd and Bolton feature on the board so don't choose to be them.
You can have as many players as you like.

Follow the instructions on the game and see if you can win the race to be Premier League champions.
For most turns you just throw the dice once and move forward from one to six squares as appropriate but when you have a game to play, such as on square 4, you'll need to throw the dice twice.
Every time you win a game move forward three spaces, if you draw a game move forward one space and if you lose stay where you are. You can win, draw or lose a game on squares 4, 9, 20 and 34 when you have to throw the dice twice to get your score and the score of the opposition. On square four for example you are away to Arsenal. The first throw is Arsenal's score and the second throw is your team's score.
The winner is the first person to reach square 38.

1.
Throw a three to begin with three points and move to square three or a one to begin on square one.

2.

3.

6.
You sign a top striker just before the Transfer Window closes. Move forward six spaces.

9.
You face Newcastle away. Throw both dice, the first one is Newcastle's score, the second one is yours. If Newcastle win have another go. It's a Sunderland annual after all!

12.

4.

Your first very difficult game of the season, Arsenal away. Throw the dice twice, the first throw is Arsenal's score, the second throw is yours.

7.

10.

13.
You have a key player sent off in a vital game. Miss a turn – you're suspended.

5.

8.
Both of your goalies are injured in the same game. Go back a space.

11.

14.

15.

Name five Premier League teams whose home kit is blue. If you can do that move forward an extra space.

21.

27.

Fixture pile ups cause problems. Throw a five or miss a turn.

33.

All your closest rivals lose. Go forward two spaces.

16.

22.

Your best midfielder has been sold in the January Transfer window. Go back to square 17.

28.

34.

You play Bolton without five first choice players. Roll the dice twice. The first one is yours and the second is Bolton's – but Bolton's score counts double.

17.

29.

35.

18.

Opponents have games in hand on you. Miss two turns.

24.

30.

36.

19.

You are half way through the season. Throw the dice twice and if both throws are the same (eg two fours) then have an extra turn.

25.

You get a last minute penalty with the score at 1-1. Have an extra throw and if it is a ONE then you've scored and can go forward three squares.

31.

You concede a last minute penalty. If the player on your left can name ten Sunderland players you have to go back to square 21.

37.

Sing the tune of 'Match of the Day' or miss a turn.

20.

Man Utd at home. Throw the dice twice, the first score is yours, the second is Man Utd's.

26.

32.

Two of your best players are injured on international duty. Miss a turn.

38.

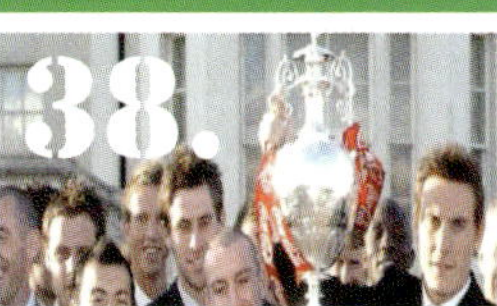

Congratulations. If you are the first player to reach no 38 you are the winner!

SUNSHINELAND

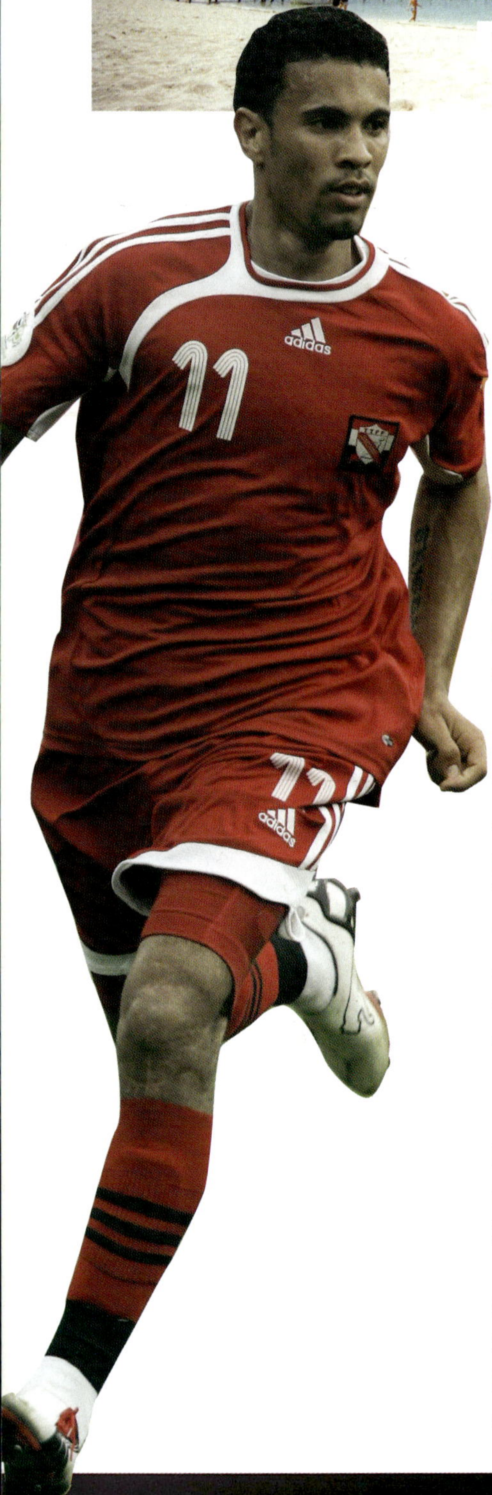

With an Irish Chairman, manager, owners, players and fans Sunderland obviously have a big Irish influence at the club but there is also a massive influence from the other side of the Atlantic Ocean. With three players from Trinidad and Tobago Sunderland became 'Sunshineland' as the Caribbean trio helped put smiles on everyone's faces.

Dwight Yorke is famous for having the nicest smile in football and when he gave up soccer in Sydney in Australia's 'A' league to come back to play in England it was a big plus to Roy Keane's plans to get Sunderland back into the Premier League.
The next transfer window saw two of Yorkie's Trinidad and Tobago team mates from the 2006 World Cup finals join him in the north east. Carlos Edwards and Stern John (who has played over 100 times for his country) signed up and brought a touch of sunshine to Sunderland.

"It is great for Trinidad football to have Dwight, Carlos and Stern back in the Premier League with Sunderland and we are all now following the club with special interest" says T & T spokesman Shaun Fuentes.

Supporters of Trinidad and Tobago have even travelled to Sunderland to cheer the Lads on and Sunderland supporters have shown how much they think of the Caribbean comrades by creating their own SAFC Soca Warriors banner.

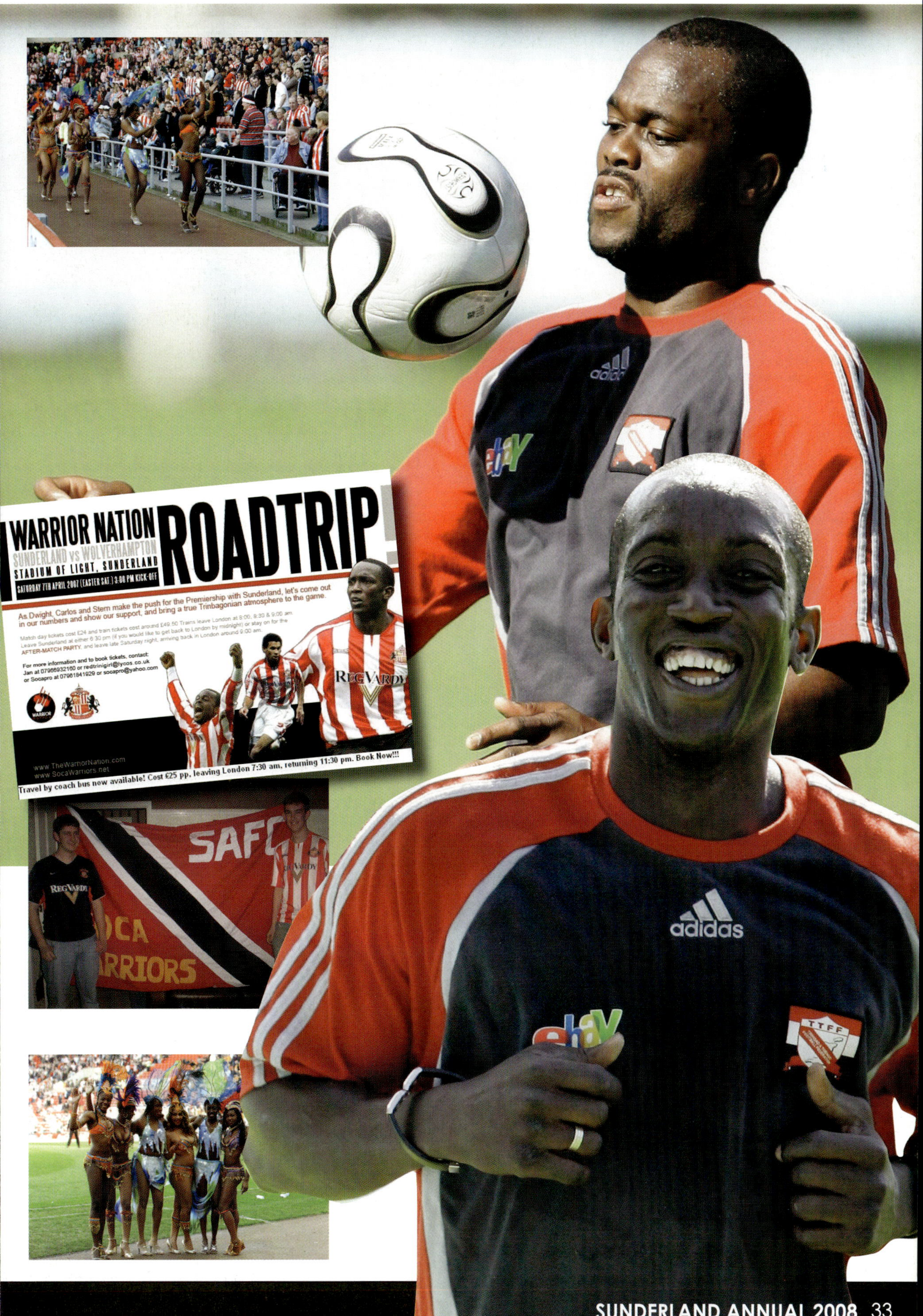

WARRIOR NATION ROADTRIP!
SUNDERLAND vs WOLVERHAMPTON
STADIUM OF LIGHT, SUNDERLAND
SATURDAY 7TH APRIL 2007 (EASTER SAT.) 3:00 PM KICK-OFF
As Dwight, Carlos and Stern make the push for the Premiership with Sunderland, let's come out in our numbers and show our support, and bring a true Trinbagonian atmosphere to the game.
Match day tickets cost £24 and train tickets cost around £49.50 Trains leave London at 8:00, 8:30 & 9:00 am Leave Sunderland at either 6:30 pm (if you would like to get back to London by midnight) or stay on for the AFTER-MATCH PARTY, and leave late Saturday night, arriving back in London around 9:00 am.
For more information and to book tickets, contact:
Jan at 07956932160 or redtrinigirl@lycos.co.uk
or Socapro at 07961841929 or socapro@yahoo.com
www.TheWarriorNation.com
www.SocaWarriors.net
Travel by coach bus now available! Cost £25 pp, leaving London 7:30 am, returning 11:30 pm. Book Now!!!
REG VARDY

SUNDIRELAND

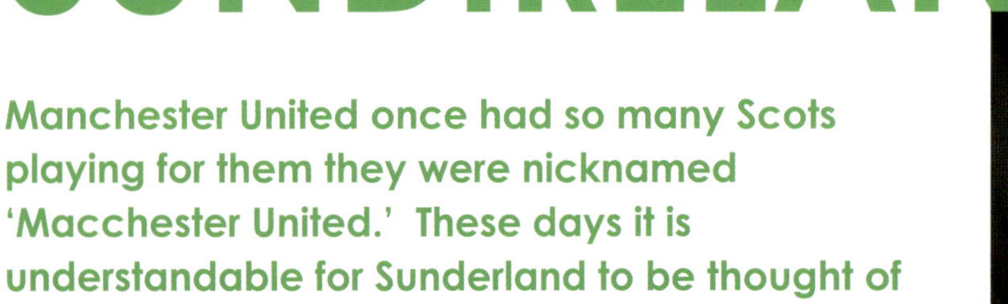

Manchester United once had so many Scots playing for them they were nicknamed 'Macchester United.' These days it is understandable for Sunderland to be thought of as 'Sundireland' because of the tremendous links that exist between Sunderland and Ireland.

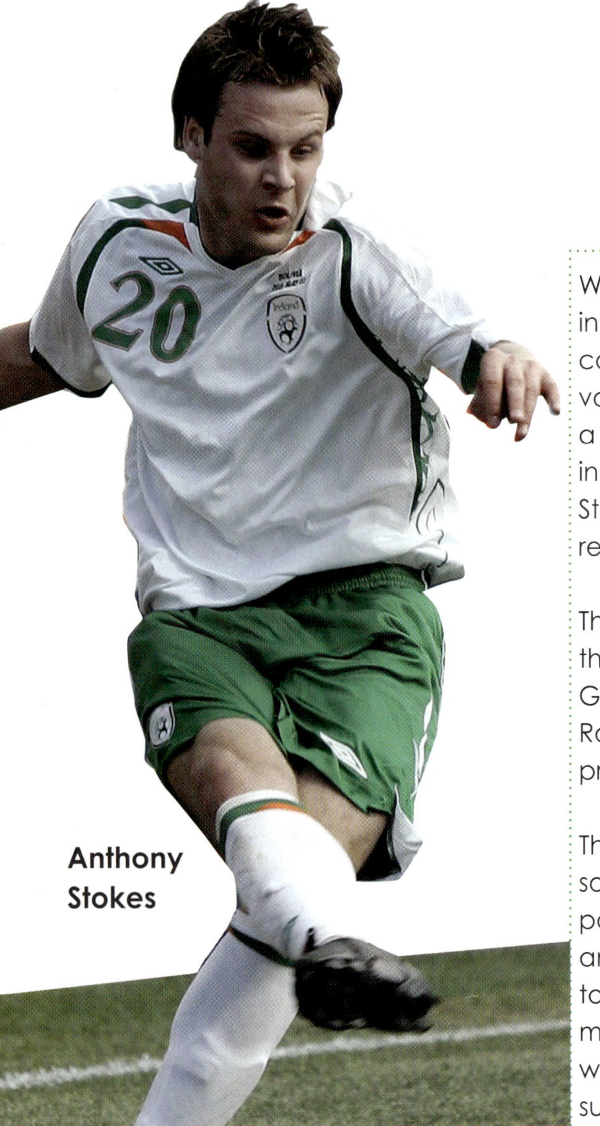

Anthony Stokes

With an Irish chairman in Niall Quinn, an Irish manager in Roy Keane, mainly Irish owners in the Drumaville consortium, Irish sponsors in Boylesports, an Irishman voted 'Player of the Century' in Charlie Hurley and a host of Irish players and managers in recent years including Daryl Murphy and Anthony Stokes, Sunderland are proud of their relationship with the Emerald Isle.

The club even went on a tour of Ireland in the summer playing games in Dublin, Cork and Galway while St. Patrick's Athletic and Shamrock Rovers sent teams to play at Sunderland when it was pre-season in Ireland.

The people of Sunderland and the north east have so much in common with Irish folk that it is a perfect pairing. They all love their sport, they all love partying and socialising and they are known for being down to earth and always ready to help a friend. With more and more Irish supporters travelling over to watch games at the Stadium of Light and Sunderland supporters loving their trips across the Irish Sea, 'Sundireland' is a partnership set to be as effective as Phillips and Quinn once were up front.

Liam Miller

Shelbourne
v
Sunderland

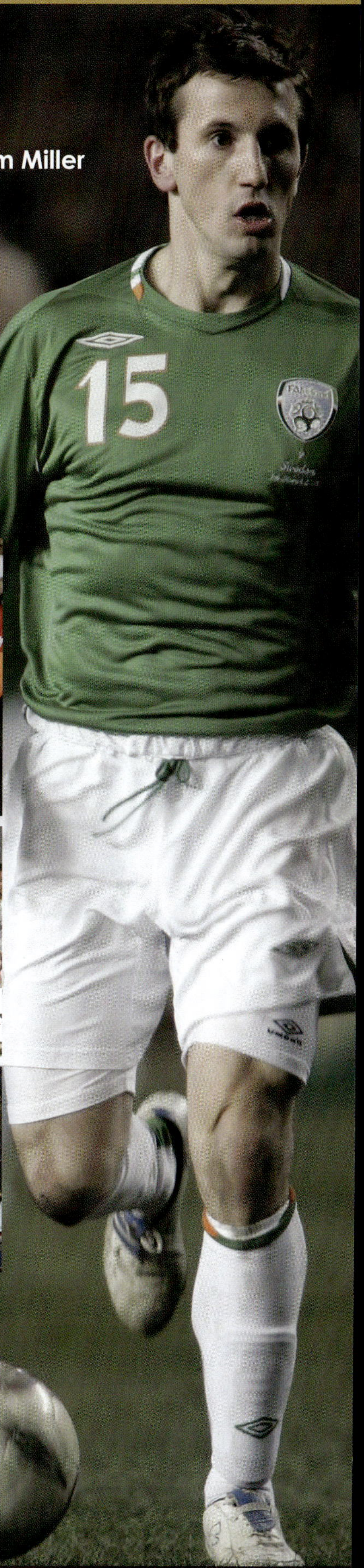

David
Connolly

ON YER BIKE!

'Climbing to the top

Training is never dull at Sunderland. The players do a lot of work with the ball and from time to time come into training to find a surprise is in store for them. A day mountain biking around the North Yorks Dales in Swaledale was one such surprise. Asked to just get their training shoes and get on the coach the first team squad set off for a day on two wheels. "We sometimes try to do things away from the training ground and I think the players enjoyed it. It's important to do things like that" explained Roy Keane.

David Connolly and Toby Hysen head the group

Split into teams the players set off on a race with each section of the competition being followed by a skills challenge that had to be completed before moving on to the next stage. It was hard fought training because no footballer likes losing at anything but it was skipper Dean Whitehead's team that came out as champions.

'Carlos' Edwards reverts to his bike.

Stephen Elliott doesn't look happy!

Toby rides one handed.

Carlos Edwards chases Jonny Evans

SAFC.COM ...
SUNDERLAND AFC ON THE WEB

safc.com is Sunderland AFC's official website. It is the place to go for everything SAFC.

The site covers every corner of your favourite club - news, tickets, players, matches, live commentary, pictures, history, mobile content, wallpapers, fun and games, competitions, quizzes, podcasts ... and more.

You can read on a daily basis what Roy Keane and his players are up to.

Watch videos of the Sunderland manager and of your favourite players. Relive those special matches by visiting SAFC World, our online TV channel.

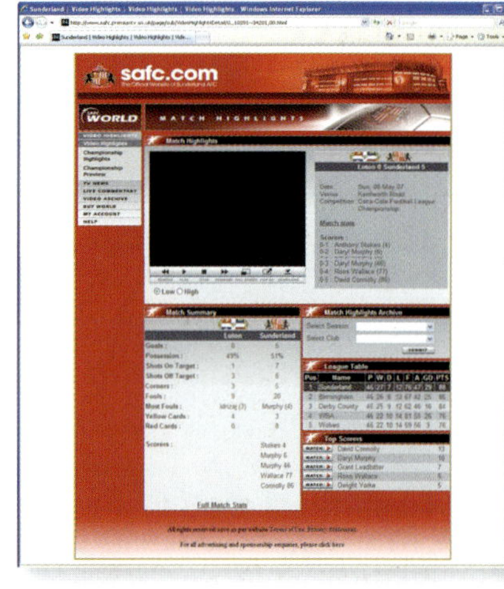

The players read the website and you can use it to ask them questions in our exclusive Q&A and live webchat features. How cool is that?

And make sure you visit the 24/7 section for lots of fun and games. This is an exclusive area of safc.com, dedicated to the club's younger fans. Meet Samson and Delilah, interview a Sunderland star, get your pictures on the site and more.

You can win top prizes every week in safc.com's competitions section - including tickets, signed shirts, balls and programmes, books and even holidays.

And don't miss the weekly SAFC Podcast with Simon Crabtree. The podcasts are great fun and you can listen to them on your computer or MP3 player.

You can even edit safc.com, sending in your news, views and pictures to be used in the SAFC Blog section, for our world of readers to see!

safc.com - the best for Sunderland AFC

```
R  O  Y  K  E  A  N  E  K  Q  T  B  V  C  J  S  G
R  D  A  Y  B  Z  I  E  A  E  F  B  Q  M  X  P  M
A  D  E  T  Y  N  A  D  R  A  W  N  E  R  R  A  D
N  A  S  A  Y  L  L  O  N  N  O  C  D  I  V  A  D
T  C  O  S  O  M  L  Y  O  F  B  A  J  S  V  U  W
H  O  E  I  W  B  Q  F  Y  N  Q  R  L  F  U  V  I
O  I  M  P  M  A  U  B  A  M  O  L  T  I  M  C  G
N  B  A  J  G  D  I  R  T  S  H  O  V  R  R  H  H
Y  N  J  S  P  C  N  E  S  X  M  S  N  U  W  A  T
S  W  R  D  E  A  N  W  H  I  T  E  H  E  A  D  Y
T  K  D  S  R  B  A  H  J  O  G  D  M  N  H  E  O
O  O  H  R  M  L  W  U  U  D  H  W  E  Y  B  I  R
K  X  S  E  L  T  Y  U  O  L  Y  A  G  C  A  L  K
E  W  R  A  W  E  R  T  Y  O  T  R  C  L  I  D  E
S  T  C  R  N  J  O  H  N  L  S  D  F  J  O  U  G
R  E  B  I  F  U  L  O  O  U  P  S  J  E  S  O  M
```

CAN YOU FIND THE FOLLOWING TEN NAMES IN THIS WORDSEARCH?

The names can be forwards, backwards, up and down and as a tough challenge
there is one that is diagonal and backwards.

ROY KEANE

NIALL QUINN

DEAN WHITEHEAD

CARLOS EDWARDS

ROSS WALLACE

DAVID CONNOLLY

DWIGHT YORKE

STERN JOHN

ANTHONY STOKES

DARREN WARD

JACK COLBACK

A player who keeps getting better and better, Jack is a physically strong midfielder from Killingworth near Newcastle. He takes penalties and scored from the spot as top spot in the league was clinched with a 1-0 win away to Man Utd.

DAVID BROWN

England U16 international full back now in his first year full time at the club, David is from Stanley in Co. Durham and has been with SAFC since the age of eight.

JORDAN COOK

Midfielder in his second year as a full time academy player, Jordan comes from Easington Lane and first joined SAFC when he was seven.

THE YOUNG ONES

Sunderland's Academy U18 team won their league last season and reached the FA Premier League Academy U18 final where they were very unlucky to lose on penalties to Leicester City after twice hitting the woodwork.

JOE CORNFORTH

The nephew of former Sunderland player John Cornforth, Joe is a centre back now in his first year at SAFC having previously played for Cramlington Juniors.

CONOR HOURIHANE

Republic of Ireland youth international left winger from Cork. Conor chose to come to Sunderland ahead of Liverpool and Celtic and is now in his first year on Wearside.

GAVIN DONOGHUE

A Republic of Ireland youth international defender, Gavin had a terrible time with injuries last season and was allowed extra time until January 2008 to try and win a professional contract.

LIAM HUBBOCK

A Newcastle born striker who used to play for Wallsend Boys' Club, Liam is now in his first year as a full time academy player at Sunderland.

JOSHUA HOME-JACKSON

A striker from Easington Village, Josh is in his second year. His first year highlights were a hat trick against his former club Middlesbrough and a goal against Manchester City in the FA Premier League Academy U18 northern final.

MARTIN HUNTER

A goalkeeper from Whitley Bay, Martin made his U18 debut at Cardiff City's Ninian Park in the FA Youth Cup in February 2007.

MICHAEL KAY

An England youth international right back from Consett in County Durham, Michael is an excellent footballer with plenty of ability and a willingness to work at his game.

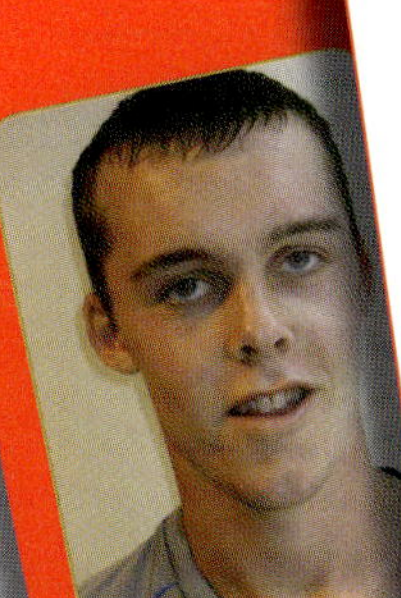

MICHAEL LIDDLE

London born and north east raised, Michael qualifies for the Republic of Ireland through his Dundalk born mother and has been capped by the Republic at U18 level.

NIALL MCARDLE

Niall is a Republic of Ireland international centre back from Malhaide in County Dublin. Currently in his second year at the club, McArdle is a defender who always tries to use the ball positively.

DAN MADDEN

A former Belmont School student from Durham, Dan is a central defender in his first year as a full time academy player.

NATHAN LUSCOMBE

An always determined left winger or left back, Nathan scored a last minute winner in last season's FA Premier League Academy U18 northern final. Carries the ball well and is fierce in the tackle.

LIAM NOBLE

Like Liam Hubbock, Noble is a former Wallsend Boys' Club player. He is a midfielder who likes to pick the ball up from his back four.

JORDAN HENDERSON

Jordan scored two great goals at the Stadium of Light last season: one direct from a corner in the FA Premier League Academy U18 final against Leicester and one with an absolute screamer against Bolton in the FA Youth Cup. He is an attacking midfielder from East Herrington in Sunderland.

GAVIN SCOTT

A former captain of the Derwentside District team, Gavin is a striker or winger from Shotley Bridge in Co. Durham.

ANDREW GALER

Sunderland born striker, Andrew appeared as a late sub last season's Northern Final against Man City when he was still at school having first played at U18 level when he was still 15.

ADAM REED

Adam is a Hartlepool born midfielder Adam has been with Sunderland since he was eight. He is now in his first year as a full time academy player.

MARTYN WAGHORN

A South Shields born striker or left winger, 'Waggy' played in a reserve game away to Liverpool when he was only 15! He is now in his second year as a full time academy player.

WISE MEN SAY

Sunderland supporters can be as noisy as any fans in the country, in fact noisier! Their loyalty is beyond question. Name another club who would average over 30,000 if they finished bottom of the league with a record low 15 points and didn't win a home game until the last home game of the season as Sunderland did two years ago?

One of the things that is special about Sunderland's supporters is the vast repertoire of songs they have. Every club's fans have their own chants but at some clubs there only seem to be about half a dozen songs that are ever heard. However when the red and white army roll into town it is like installing a juke box in the visitors' end. Perhaps it's those long coach journeys from the north east that give Sunderland's fans the edge in coming up with chants?

Some of the chants are too rude to print and many chants are aimed at teasing local rivals but some of the best ones seem to be conjured up at the spur of the moment. Take Sunderland's trip to Cardiff late last season. All season City fans had serenaded their leading scorer Michael Chopra with a version of The Automatic's 'What's that coming over the hill?' singing 'What's that coming over the hill, It's Michael Chopra, it's Michael Chopra.' Sunderland have since signed Michael Chopra who had certainly lapped up his goals that had beaten Sunderland at the Stadium of Light earlier in the season when Cardiff sat proudly at the top of the league but by now Sunderland were storming to the championship while Cardiff were fading from even having a chance of a play off place and as Sunderland inflicted City's first home defeat in almost three months the travelling fans came up with' What's that going over the hill? Is it promotion? Is it promotion?'

The same game saw the first airing of a song dedicated to player of the season, Nyron Nosworthy. The defender is a giant of a fellow and strong so to the tune of Amy Winehouse's hit 'Rehab' the lyrics were reworked as 'Try to get the ball off Nyron but he says no, no, no!' The player loved it so much he even sang it himself on the club's end of season DVD.

That wasn't the first song for Nosworthy, a version of a Gary Glitter song 'Come on Nyron' had emerged soon after Nyron arrived on a free transfer from Gillingham and needed a bit of encouragement!

There was a time when Sunderland fans could be prouder of their stadium than their team and this was indicated by the chant they came up with for many of the grounds they visited: 'My garden shed is bigger than this, my garden shed is bigger than this. It's got a door and a window, my garden shed is bigger than this!'

Like many chants that one was much copied as years before the 'Cheer Up Peter Reid' song had been of course. 'Wise Men Say' is a chant long associated with Sunderland. A reworking of an old Elvis Presley song, the title 'Wise Men Say' was the title of the first ever Sunderland fanzine in the mid 1980s and has long been the title of a page in the club's match programme.

Perhaps the best chants are the simplest and most inspirational though. Take a look at a photo of the Stadium of Light when the stands are empty and the words of the greatest of all SAFC chants is written out in the seats: "Ha'way the Lads."

CORKER – Edwards nets the goal of the season with an unbelievable, 30-yard drive – billed the greatest goal ever seen at the SoL.

HERE
WE
GOAL

When you are old enough to play a game of football with proper goals and nets for the first time there is something extra special about seeing the net bulge when the ball hits the back of it. If it's quiet you can even enjoy hearing the 'swish' the net makes as the ball thwacks into it.

Grown up footballers playing professional football are just the same. They love to score. Goals are what the game is all about. You can't win without one. Even if a game goes to penalties after a goalless draw you still have to get that ball over the line to win the game.

Strikers are judged by the number of goals they score. Sometimes they can do a great job for the team in holding up the ball and bringing other people into play but the bottom line is if they're not scoring they know they probably won't last long. Strikers who can score regularly are worth a lot of money because putting the ball in the back of the net on a regular basis is arguably the hardest job in football.

...UND THE 'KEEPER – David Connolly grabs ...nderland's second at Home Park as the Black Cats ...at Plymouth 2-0.

DRAMATIC – Grant Leadbitter nets a spectacular and crucial winner over Queen's Park Rangers at the Stadium of Light.

THAT'S A WRAP – Connolly completes a 5-0 win over Luton at Kenilworth Road on the final day of the season as Sunderland are crowned Championship champions.

CURLER – Ross Wallace bends a perfectly-placed last-minute winner against Hull at the KC Stadium.

...ANG! – Liam Miller opens his Sunderland account and ...e scoring at Elland Road in a 3-0 win over Leeds in ...rkshire.

CRUCIAL – Super striker Connolly nets a second for Sunderland at Oakwell as the Cats take a step nearer promotion with a 2-0 win over Barnsley.

CAN YOU MANAGE?

Sunderland play 38 games in the Premier League this season. There are nineteen other teams in the league and our quiz has two questions for each team – a home and away question with the away question being harder.

Award yourself three points for each question you get completely correct and one point for an answer you get partly right, e.g. if you are asked to name three players and you can only provide one or two of the names.

The answers are on page 61 and so is a copy of last season's completed Premier League table so once you have counted up your points you can see how high up the league you could manage to be.

ARSENAL

HOME: What is the name of Arsenal's stadium?

AWAY: In what year did Sunderland beat Arsenal in the semi final of the FA Cup?

ASTON VILLA

HOME: Which city is Aston Villa in?

AWAY: Which Sunderland player was once sold by Aston Villa for £12m?

BIRMINGHAM CITY

HOME: Who scored for Sunderland against Birmingham last season?

AWAY: Which team beat Birmingham on the final day of last season to enable Sunderland to overtake City and become champions?

BOLTON WANDERERS

HOME: What is Bolton's ground called?

AWAY: What is Bolton's nickname?

BLACKBURN ROVERS

HOME: Who was top scorer for Blackburn last season?

AWAY: Who did Blackburn lose to in the 2007 FA Cup semi final?

EVERTON

HOME: What is Everton's ground called?

AWAY: In which city would you find Everton?

CHELSEA

HOME: Who scored the winning goal for Chelsea in the 2007 FA Cup final?

AWAY: Until 2005 how many times had Chelsea been champions of England?

DERBY COUNTY

HOME: Who did Derby beat in the final of the 2007 Championship Play Off at Wembley?

AWAY: Which Derby player scored the first goal in Roy Keane's first match in charge of Sunderland?

FULHAM

HOME: Which former Sunderland midfielder has managed Fulham: Kevin Ball or Paul Bracewell?

AWAY: Who was the Fulham manager replaced by Lawrie Sanchez in 2007?

LIVERPOOL

HOME: Who scored Liverpool's goal in the 2007 Champions League final?

AWAY: In what year did Sunderland play Liverpool in the FA Cup final?

MANCHESTER CITY

HOME: Name the former England international sacked as City manager at the end of the 2006-07 season.

AWAY: Name the USA international midfielder Sunderland once sold to Man. City.

MIDDLESBROUGH

HOME: Before they moved to The Riverside what was Middlesbrough's previous ground called?

AWAY: How many times have Middlesbrough won the FA Cup?

MANCHESTER UTD.

HOME: Name the two players Sunderland took on loan from Manchester United last season.

AWAY: Which of the following players have NOT played for both Sunderland and Manchester Utd: Jonny Evans, Danny Simpson, Ross Wallace, Liam Miller, Gavin McCann and Dwight Yorke.

PORTSMOUTH

HOME: What is Portsmouth's nickname?

AWAY: Which of the following players have not played for Portsmouth: Linvoy Primus, David James, Matthew Taylor, Pascal Chimbonda, Pedro Mendes and Ben Foster.

WIGAN ATHLETIC

HOME: Which two players did Sunderland sign from Wigan last season?

AWAY: Name the winger Sunderland sold to Everton in 2003 who later signed for Wigan.

NEWCASTLE UTD.

HOME: Which former Sunderland player became Newcastle manager in 2007?

AWAY: Which former Newcastle player was manager of Sunderland when Sunderland won the FA Cup in 1973?

WEST HAM UNITED

HOME: Who did Sunderland sell to West Ham last season?

AWAY: Who did Sunderland sign from West Ham last season?

TOTTENHAM HOTSPUR

HOME: Who did Sunderland sign from Spurs last season?

AWAY: Who did Sunderland sell to Spurs last season?

READING

HOME: Which record of Sunderland's did Reading beat in 2005-06?

AWAY: Which former Sunderland and Everton winger played for Reading in 2007?

RED AND WHITE DYNAMITE

OLYMPIAKOS

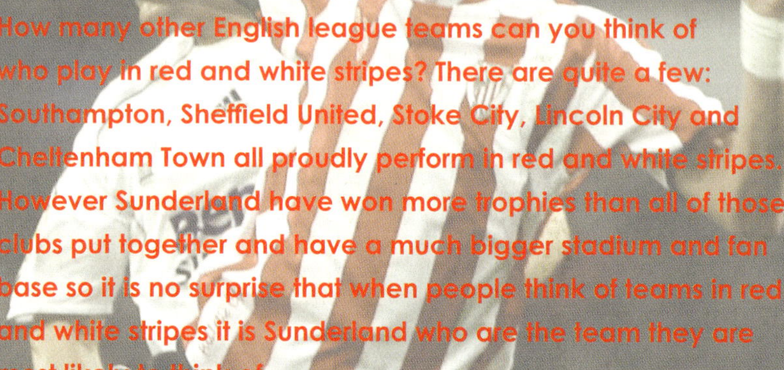

Lots of teams from around the world also wear red and white stripes. In the case of Athletic Bilbao in Spain they wear Sunderland's colours because they were formed by a man from Sunderland, Arthur Pentland who first travelled to Bilbao in 1894, four years before Athletic (note they call themselves Athletic not Athletico) were formed. Athletico Madrid wore red and white stripes because they were originally loaned a set of strips by Athletic Bilbao so in a way Sunderland were responsible for their colours too.

ATHLETIC BILBAO

Athletic Bilbao have been champions of Spain eight times, one less than Athletico Madrid. Other giant European teams to wear red and white stripes include:

PSV Eindhoven, 15 times champions of Holland and former European Cup winners.
Sparta Rotterdam: 6 times champions of Holland
Olympiakos: 29 times champions of Greece
FC Nurnberg: 9 times champions of Germany
Red Star Belgrade: 29 times champions of the former Yugoslavia and former European Cup winners.

Did you know: In their early years Newcastle United's colours were...red and white stripes?

The Stadium of Light is one of the best grounds in the Premier League. Even when there isn't a match on the ground is worth visiting because there is so much to see both inside and outside the stadium.

1.

The first thing you see when you drive up to the stadium is this giant miner's lamp which is on a roundabout outside SAFC's main reception. This 'Davy Lamp' pays tribute to the fact that the Stadium of Light is built on what was Wearmouth Colliery, once one of the biggest pits in the country.

2.

Outside the massive West Stand you can see this model pit wheel. You can see a colliery winding gear wheel at the top of Sunderland's club badge. Once again this is in honour of the club's mining heritage.

3.

Just outside the main entrance to the stadium is the fans' statue. This was the first statue to be erected at the ground. It shows three generations of Sunderland supporters on their way to the match. Supporting Sunderland is very much a family thing. It is in the blood of generations of supporters.

4.

As you approach the stadium on foot from the city centre – as most fans do on matchdays – you see the Stokoe Statue. Bob Stokoe was Sunderland's manager when the Lads sensationally won the FA Cup against hot favourites Leeds in 1973. The statue shows Stokoe running to greet goalkeeper Jimmy Montgomery as the final whistle was blown on that glorious Wembley afternoon.

5.

The entrance hall of the Stadium of Light features the world's biggest and oldest oil painting of a football match. It shows Sunderland playing Aston Villa in 1895, just a few hundred yards away from the Stadium of Light.

6.

Having a look inside the dressing rooms is one of the highlights of being on a stadium tour.

7.

Running down the players' tunnel can't be beaten if you want to imagine what it's like to be a professional player. On the stadium tour they even play the famous entrance music while you run out!

8.

The Stadium of Light has loads of places where people can have something to eat and drink at the ground. One of the best places is the Black Cats' Bar. You can take a tour of the Stadium of Light on any day except Christmas Day. Ring 0191 551 5055 to book a place.

FOOTBALL PROGRAMMES

HOW TO START A COLLECTION

There is one thing that makes your memory of a football match very special and that is a match programme. Buying one at every game you go to is a brilliant way of being able to look back and remember all of the matches you have attended. Go to games for a few years and it's always interesting to look at old programmes and see what was said about Sunderland players when they were playing for other teams. You can plot the changing hairstyles, the footballing fashions and see what people were saying about the Lads at the time. A look at the Academy pages makes you think there are some players who have disappeared totally but it's always fascinating to read about players like Grant Leadbitter years before he made it to the first team.

Some people collect programmes from every game they go to. For lots of people that's not enough. They try to get every Sunderland programme from as far back in history as possible or at least since they were born. Even one programme per season from your birth makes a cracking collection.

Buying programmes from away matches is another way to build up a history of your club. Obviously away programmes are mostly about the team whose home game it is but it's always good to read what they say about Sunderland players.

Some collectors like to specialise in a particular kind of programme such as FA Cup ties, cup finals, internationals, first programme of a season, derby game programmes and so on.

Starting a collection is easy. Lots of programme dealers (you'll see them advertised in football magazines) make cheap offers of bundles of programmes to get young collectors started and the Sunderland Supporters' Association just over the road from the Stadium of Light in Monk Street almost always have special cheap offers on bundles of old Sunderland programmes.

Old programmes can be worth a lot of money, some really rare ones can be worth over £1000! So if your grandad has a cupboard full of old Sunderland programmes ask him to show you them and be careful with them!

Modern day programmes are much bigger and glossier than programmes from years ago. These days you can expect Sunderland's programme 'Red and White' to have exclusive interviews with Roy Keane, Niall Quinn and Dean Whitehead in every issue as well as a host of other interviews including ones with the referee, someone from the visiting team, an old Sunderland player and an academy player who might be a star of the future.

Take a look in the club shop at the programmes next time you visit the Stadium of Light and start your collection.

WHERE IN THE WORLD?

Can you match the footballer to the country he is from?

Carlos Edwards	Hungary
Anthony Stokes	Trinidad and Tobago
Dean Whitehead	Wales
Darren Ward	Republic of Ireland
Toby Hysen	England
Marton Fulop	Sweden

WHO AM I?

Try and work out the answer using as few clues as possible.

1. I was born in the year Sunderland last won the FA Cup.
2. I played in the League Cup final in 2006.
3. I am an international footballer.
4. I have played in Wales as well as England.
5. My first club in England was Middlesbrough.

GLOBE TROTTERS

Sunderland have played all of these teams in recent years.
Can you match the team to the country?

Charleston Battery	Spain
Vancouver Whitecaps	USA
Seville	France
Calais	Republic of Ireland
Royal Antwerp	Holland
Cork City	Belgium
Vitesse Arnhem	Canada

SUNDERLAND 5 – 2 MANCHESTER UNITED

All five of these players have played for Sunderland but can you name the two who have also played for Manchester United?

SUNDERLAND   MANCHESTER UNITED

ON THE BALL

Can you name the three teams hidden on these footballs?

GONE MISSING

Fill in the missing letters to come up with the name of former Sunderland players.

1) _ _ e _ e   _ a _ _ _ e l _

2) _ _ a _   _ a _ _ _ _ e

3) _ _ o _ _ _   _ _ a _ _ n _ _

CORNERED

Can you identify the four players from the pictures below?

Footballers like being in the fast lane so Sunderland's squad put themselves to the test with their very own go karting championships. First of all the players were given a safety demonstration and then got down to the task of showing who was the Lewis Hamilton of the squad with a fiercely contested competition where midfielder Liam Miller proved he was the driving force of the club.

WATER SLIDES

Skipper Dean Whitehead, Republic of Ireland international Daryl Murphy and Sweden international Toby Hysen are coming into the best years of their careers so they could afford to go watersliding on a trip to Portugal without needing to worry about any newspapers claiming they were 'on the slide'. Roy Keane likes his squad to try unusual things and so as part of a warm weather training trip to Portugal the lads got their swimming costumes on and had a great time!

RED AND WHITE · RECORDS

Sunderland have won the FA Cup twice, in 1937 and 1973. The 1973 win was one of the most famous cup finals of all time.

Sunderland have been champions of England six times, only Liverpool, Manchester United, Arsenal, Everton and Aston Villa have been champions more times.

Sunderland's highest ever attendance is 75,118. That is almost 7000 more than any other north east club have ever had.

Sunderland's all time top goalscorer is Bobby Gurney who scored 228 goals for the lads.

Sunderland have won the League Championship trophy four times since 1996.

The Stadium of Light is the biggest football ground built in England in the second half of the 20th century.

In 1912-13 Sunderland were champions and got to the FA Cup final in the same season.

Sunderland's previous ground Roker Park staged three group games and a quarter final when the World Cup was held in England.

In the Millennium season, Kevin Phillips scored 30 goals in 36 Premier League games and became the only Englishman ever to win the European Golden Shoe as the continent's top scorer.

Davie Halliday is Sunderland's top scorer in one season: he netted 43 in 1928-29.

Charlie Hurley was named Sunderland's 'Player of the Century' in the club's Centenary Year of 1979. He is also Sunderland's most capped player, winning 38 caps for the Republic of Ireland while with Sunderland.

Four players have scored five goals in a game for Sunderland: Jimmy Millar, Charlie Buchan, Bobby Gurney and Nick Sharkey.

Sunderland chairman Niall Quinn won 81 of his 91 Republic of Ireland caps while with Sunderland and at the time of his retirement was his country's all time record goalscorer.

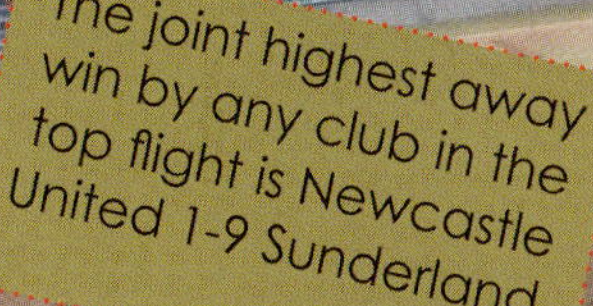

The joint highest away win by any club in the top flight is Newcastle United 1-9 Sunderland.

Sunderland's record appearance maker is Jimmy Montgomery. Altogether 'Monty' made 627 competitive appearances for Sunderland.

The world's first ever £1,000 transfer was in 1905 when Sunderland sold Alf Common to Middlesbrough.

Goalkeeper Derek Forster was just 15 years and 185 days old when he played in the top flight for Sunderland against Leicester in 1964. He is still the youngest goalkeeper to have played at the top level. In the opposition goal was Gordon Banks who would win the World Cup with England two years later.

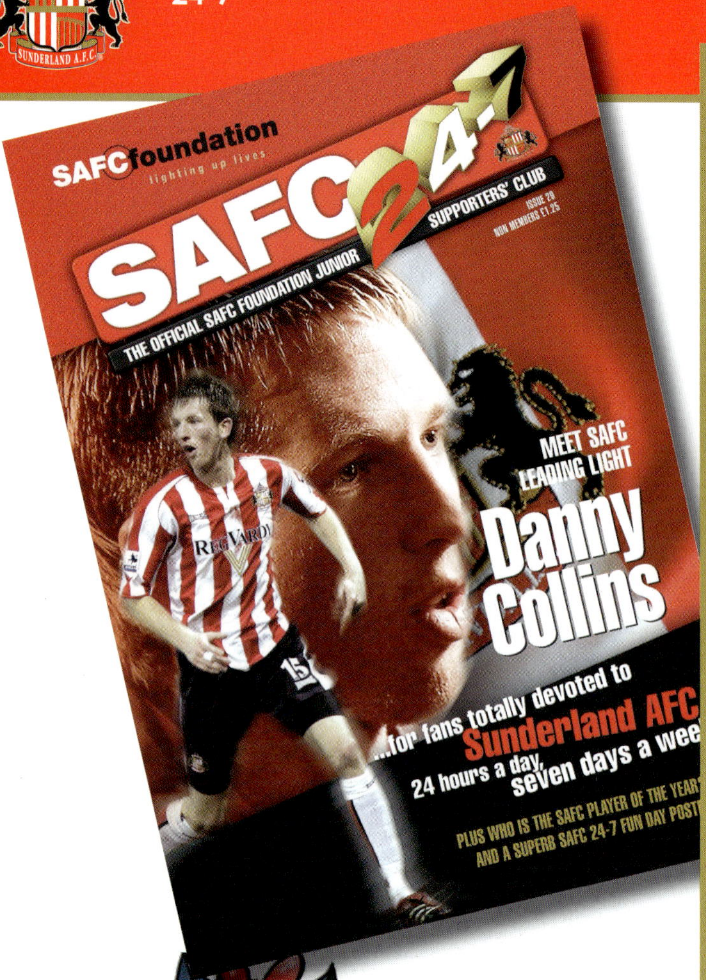

24-7

Sunderland supporters don't just support their team on the day of a match. They live and breathe all things red and white and that is why Sunderland's junior supporters' club is called 24-7... because Sunderland supporters support their team 24 hours a day 7 days a week.

Any young supporter can join 24-7. All you have to do is log on to safc. com and click on the 24-7 section. There is a special section on safc.com for 24-7 members and there is also a great magazine just for 24-7 members. You can even volunteer to help club mascots Samson and Delilah to write the magazine by writing in to volunteer to go to the training ground and interview a player.

24-7 member Sophie White found out from Carlos Edwards that he grew up as an AC Milan fan and that Nyron Nosworthy is his best friend at Sunderland. Another 24-7 member, Stuart Littlemore interviewed Ross Wallace who told him that he has a pet hamster, wants to be a manager or coach one day and grew up supporting Celtic. If you would like to be a 24-7 magazine reporter for a day, join up and contact 24-7 magazine to volunteer. Who knows, one day Samson might give you a call!

	P	W	D	L	F	A	W	D	L	F	A	PTS
Man Utd	38	15	2	2	46	12	13	3	3	37	15	89
Chelsea	38	12	7	0	37	11	12	4	3	27	13	83
Liverpool	38	14	4	1	39	7	6	4	9	18	20	68
Arsenal	38	12	6	1	43	16	7	5	7	20	19	68
Tottenham	38	12	3	4	34	22	5	6	8	23	32	60
Everton	38	11	4	4	33	17	4	9	6	19	19	58
Bolton	38	9	5	5	26	20	7	3	9	21	32	56
Reading	38	11	2	6	29	20	5	5	9	23	27	55
Portsmouth	38	11	5	3	28	15	3	7	9	17	27	54
Blackburn	38	9	3	7	31	25	6	4	9	21	29	52
Aston Villa	38	7	8	4	20	14	4	9	6	23	27	50
Middlesbro	38	10	3	6	31	24	2	7	10	13	25	46
Newcastle	38	7	7	5	23	20	4	3	12	15	27	43
Man City	38	5	6	8	10	16	6	3	10	19	28	42
West Ham	38	8	2	9	24	26	4	3	12	11	33	41
Fulham	38	7	7	5	18	18	1	8	10	20	42	39
Wigan	38	5	4	10	18	30	5	4	10	19	29	38
Sheff Utd	38	7	6	6	24	21	3	2	14	8	34	38
Charlton	38	7	5	7	19	20	1	5	13	15	40	34
Watford	38	3	9	7	19	25	2	4	13	10	34	28

```
O Y K E A N E K Q T B V C J S G
D A Y B Z I E A E F B Q M X P M
D E T Y N A D R A W N E R R A D
A S A Y L L O N N O C D I V A D
C O S O M L Y O F B A J S V U W
O E I W B Q F Y N Q R L F U V I
I M P M A U B A M O L T I M C G
B A J G D I R T S H O V R R H H
N J S P C N E S X M S N U W A T
W R D E A N W H I T E H E A D Y
K D S R B A H J O G D M N H E O
O H R M L W U U D H W E Y B I R
X S E L T Y U O L Y A G C A L K
W R C W E R T Y O T R C L I D E
T E R N J O H N L S D F J O U G
O B I F U L O O U P S J E S O M
```

CAN YOU MANAGE ANSWERS

Can you manage to get over 89 points and beat Man Utd to the title? If you got 68 and finished in the top four, well done you are good enough to qualify for the Champions League. How about 56 to finish 7th or above and make it into the UEFA Cup? That's a good performance. If you got between 55 and 44 to finish in mid table then you have the basis to become a good expert. Between 43 and 39 just to avoid relegation then you need to work a bit harder to improve. Less than 39 and in the bottom three then pick yourself up, keep learning about the game and aim to improve next time.

ARSENAL
HOME: The Emirates Stadium.
AWAY: 1973

ASTON VILLA
HOME: Birmingham.
AWAY: Dwight Yorke

BIRMINGHAM CITY
HOME: Carlos Edwards.
AWAY: Preston North End.

BLACKBURN ROVERS
HOME: Benny McCarthy.
AWAY: Chelsea.

BOLTON WANDERERS
HOME: The Reebok Stadium.
AWAY: The Trotters.

CHELSEA
HOME: Didier Drogba.
AWAY: Once.

DERBY COUNTY
HOME: West Brom
AWAY: Matt Oakley

EVERTON
HOME: Goodison Park.
AWAY: Liverpool.

FULHAM
HOME: Paul Bracewell.
AWAY: Chris Coleman.

LIVERPOOL
HOME: Dirk Kuyt
AWAY: 1992.

MANCHESTER CITY
HOME: Stuart Pearce.
AWAY: Claudio Reyna.

MANCHESTER UNITED
HOME: Jonny Evans and Danny Simpson.
AWAY: Ross Wallace and Gavin McCann.

MIDDLESBROUGH
HOME: Ayresome Park
AWAY: None.

NEWCASTLE UNITED
HOME: Sam Allardyce.
AWAY: Bob Stokoe.

PORTSMOUTH
HOME: Pompey
AWAY: Pascal Chimbonda and Ben Foster.

READING
HOME: Most points won in a season.
AWAY: John Oster.

TOTTENHAM HOTSPUR
HOME: Marton Fulop
AWAY: Ben Alnwick.

WEST HAM UNITED
HOME: George McCartney.
AWAY: Clive Clarke.

WIGAN ATHLETIC
HOME: David Connolly and Graham Kavanagh.
AWAY: Kevin Kilbane.

ANSWERS from pages 54 and 55

WHERE IN THE WORLD?
Carlos Edwards – Trinidad and Tobago
Anthony Stokes – Republic of Ireland
Dean Whitehead – England
Darren Ward – Wales
Toby Hysen – Sweden
Marton Fulop – Hungary

WHO AM I?
Graham Kavanagh

GLOBE TROTTERS
Charleston Battery – USA
Vancouver Whitecaps – Canada
Seville – Spain
Calais – France
Royal Antwerp –Belgium
Cork City – Republic of Ireland
Vitesse Arnhem – Holland

**SUNDERLAND 5-2
MANCHESTER UNITED**
Dwight Yorke
Liam Miller

ON THE BALL
1)   Everton
2)   Aston Villa
3)   Derby County

GONE MISSING
1)   Steve Caldwell
2)   Liam Lawrence
3)   George McCartney

CORNERED
Stephen Elliott
Jake Richardson
Ross Wallace
David Connolly